JULY

KATHLEEN OSSIP

SARABANDE BOOKS
Louisville, KY

Publisher's Cataloging-In-Publication Data
(Prepared by The Donohue Group, Inc.)

Names: Ossip, Kathleen, author.
Title: July / by Kathleen Ossip.
Description: Louisville, KY : Sarabande Books, 2021
Some poems previously published in various literary and news magazines.
Identifiers: ISBN 9781946448781 | ISBN 9781946448798 (e-book)
Subjects: LCSH: United States—Description and travel—Poetry.
Mothers and daughters—Travel—United States—Poetry.
United States—Politics and government—21st century—Poetry.
United States—Social life and customs—21st century—Poetry.
Ossip, Kathleen—Diaries. | American poetry. | LCGFT: Poetry. | Diaries.
Classification: LCC PS3615.S6 J85 2021 (print) | LCC PS3615.S6 (e-book) | DDC 811/.6—dc23

Cover and interior design by Alban Fischer.
Printed in Canada.
This book is printed on acid-free paper.
Sarabande Books is a nonprofit literary organization.

   [clmp]

This project is supported in part by an award from the National Endowment for the Arts.
The Kentucky Arts Council, the state arts agency, supports Sarabande Books with
state tax dollars and federal funding from the National Endowment for the Arts.

for Muriel

CONTENTS

ACKNOWLEDGMENTS

Thank you to the editors of these journals, which first published some of the poems:

Academy of American Poets *Poem-a-Day*, *Bennington Review*, *American Poetry Review*, *The Baffler*, *The Nation*, *Sewanee Review*, *Poetry*, *Harvard Review*, *Prac Crit*, *At Length*, *Plume*, *On the Seawall*, *The Believer*, *Kenyon Review*, *No News Today*, *The New Republic*.

Endless gratitude to the Radcliffe Institute for Advanced Study, Harvard University, for providing a nurturing environment where much of the book was written.

Also to friends who improved some poems with their generous readings: Jonathan Farmer, Heather Treseler, Rebecca Morgan Frank, David Blair, Barbara Fischer. Thanks to David Trinidad for pointing me to diary poems (and inspiring me with his), and to Geoffrey Nutter for his daylong workshop, where I used his magical pile of source materials to write a few of the poems.

Sarabande Books deserves the gratitude of anyone who cares about the health of poetry. Working with Sarah Gorham, Danika Isdahl, Kristen Renee Miller, Joanna Englert, Alban Fischer, and Emma Aprile made me feel, always, that this book could be its best self.

OCCASIONS

GO

It is a cube, it is red, it is mountainous,
it is a bird of fire, it is the bones of the pelvis, it is a walnut,
it is treasured. It is yellow Saturn wobbling in its orbit.
It is danger, squawking.

It is the desire to sit down with strangers in cafés
and then it is the strangers in cafés,
it is the man with the black T-shirt
labeled UNARMED CIVILIAN and it is the unseeing man with him

and his painful trembling.
Always it is oxygen and more oxygen. It is the fight in you
and the fight in you dying. It is the need for water
and the water that falls from the sky.

It is desperate for a theory and it is the acts you call evil
when you know that inside evil is always desperation.
It is bravery, arrogance, purpose.
It is the pink morning and your smile in the pink morning.

It is a phantom and the thin neck of a tree it
is a little project called loving the world.
It is howling in the dirt it is an extravaganza.
It's the abandoned sports bra, in the dirt beside howling you.

It's the windchimes in the thin-necked tree and
it is tonguetied. It is asleep.
It is waking up now. It is a small cat on the bed.
It is the threads of a leaf and it is the Three Graces:

Splendor, Mirth, and Good Cheer.
It is their heartfelt advice:
You can't let it hurt you.
You must let it hurt you.

It is a careless error and the hotel pool blue with chemistry.
It's a kiss of course it is a kiss.
It's an old strange book newly acquired
but not yet catalogued, it is crazy.

It is you, crazy with honesty and crazy with ambition.
It's the sun that stuns over and over again.
It's your tablet, which is every tablet everywhere.
It's an explosion it is every explosion everywhere.

It is pavement, mineral and hot and wet with droplets.
It's the stars that pitch white needles into the pond.
It is provable, it is a lotion, it is a lie.
It is a baby because everyone is a baby.

It talks to you, always to you, it moves
swiftly, it is stuck, it moves swiftly, it is stuck, it moves
swiftly. It's the impenetrable truth, now clear as ice.
It is serious, it is irreversible, it is going, going.

It is flying now flying strong enough to know anything.

BLUEBIRD

Today I sing in
a green and golden place.
My little eyes blink
in my little blue face.

My little song says
Truly truly.
The cat sits watching
coolly coolly

and no one minds if
I'm she or him
and my little heart beating
dee-dim dee-dim.

ON BOREDOM

One Saturday (Saturday!
When my time comes, among
my last thoughts will be of how
I did not fully appreciate
Saturdays!), my Aunt Anne,
who died this month, took me
to my first Broadway show:
Fiddler on the Roof.
She took me and five cousins
on an early morning bus
from the Albany Trailways station
to Port Authority.
She treated us to lunch
and then to a matinée.

I ate fried chicken for lunch
(a food I now abhor
for reasons of taste and ethics,
neither of my willed doing
but products of the passage
of time and consciousness;
then, I was beguiled
by the red plastic basket
where the golden chicken rested)
and had an orange drink and
Junior Mints in the theater.
Of the show I remember
"Matchmaker, Matchmaker" and how
the three daughters found their matches,
true love which of course came
with the iconic problems
(money, religion, politics)—

but we, the audience, knew
an inescapable pair
when we saw it. I was only
nine but wished that I
could be a pair too.
What a limited life I had.
I was nine. I didn't

know any Jews (though I'd
later marry a Jew
who has sheltered me
from iconic problems,
who has worked so I could work
on poems that don't earn money).

Sitting in the dark
full of fried chicken and
sweetness made me drowsy
and dull, my critical sense,
such as it was at nine,
absolutely dulled.
(To this day I can't sit
in a theater and feel
anything but grateful
to the actors and musicians;
I have no critical sense.)
This was not the kind
of boredom I had felt
the year before at the
Baseball Hall of Fame,
where my father (Aunt Anne's
brother, who has seen
me through life to this day:
has cushioned me through)
led me around a room
filled with nothing more
entertaining than
three walls of bronze plaques.

This was not that kind
of boredom: it was boredom
of my willed doing, abstracted
extravagance, a red-
velvet-cushioned cocoon
of mindlessness. (This sump-
tuous mindlessness
is what I cultivate
when I let a poem begin.)

Unlike the show's three daughters,
Aunt Anne was not a pair.

She was an unmarried woman,
considered pitiable
in that family and
at that time. She lived
all her life with her parents
and, after they died, alone.
She enjoyed theater and gambling
(also took me to
my first bingo night)
and vivid conversations
around her mother's kitchen
table (later hers).
Every Sunday there
I was, bored by the
grownup talk and breathing
secondhand cigarette smoke.

What a limited life she had.
With her Fire and Ice
lipstick and heavy gold bangles,
didn't she have ambitions?
I think she was ambitious
to take six kids all that way.
(Must ambition be performance?
Does ambition only count
if many people see—
"many" needs defining—
and if the people aren't
your immediate family?)

After the show, we boarded
a crowded Trailways bus
back home. We kids were sleepy,
wired, and fractious. The seats
in pairs, I had to sit
next to a stranger, a man
who looked, to a nine-year-old
who didn't know any professors,
like a professor. He wore
dark-framed glasses (like
my father's), a tweed cap.
The little pinpoint light
shone down on him. He read

first a magazine
and then a book. He had
a leather briefcase full
of books and magazines.

I had nothing to read
but my *Playbill*. I read
front to back, then back
to front, then started over
again. The man, although
absorbed in his own reading,
must have noticed because
he took the magazine
(*National Geographic*)
out from his briefcase and
gave it to me. "Maybe
you'd like to read this?"
He smiled.

        (In *Citizen Kane*,
a movie I watched with my father
and which didn't bore me,
Mr. Bernstein talks about seeing
a woman in a white
dress one day when he
was seventeen and then
never again BUT
"Not a month goes by
that I don't think of her."
This is supposed to be
a doleful mystery—
"He only saw her once!"
It's not mysterious.
It is perfectly clear.
The woman was his creation.
He conjured her from boredom.
Clarity, what use
are you to me now!
My mystery is this:
how many days were blank
of thought about Aunt Anne
who gave me this memory-poem
or about my father

who gave me leisure to think
about my inner life
instead of about
hardships and displacement.
Leisure to be bored.
Boredom is a withdrawal
of attention. Pay attention!)

My aunt and cousins in
the back of the bus were sleeping,
snuffling close but separate,
dreaming privately,
thrilling dreams probably
for dreams are never boring,
unlike the magazine
so kindly offered but
(photo of bleak hot desert,
photo of frozen mountain)
so boring. My eyes were dim
with sleepiness and the strain
of reading in the dark
and something else, a look
I carry to this day,
(no matter what I'm reading,
even when I'm reading),
that says (*Hungry, hungry!*)
"Please, won't you give me
something to read?"

CHAYOTE

is an edible plant
belonging to the gourd
family. Like other gourds,
chayote has a sprawling habit
and should only be planted if
there is plenty of room in the
garden. Chayote is originally
native to Mesoamerica—a regional
and cultural area extending from
central Mexico to Belize, Guatemala,
El Salvador, Honduras, Nicaragua, and
northern Costa Rica—which some sources
refer to in the past tense; for others, it is very
much present. The plant was first recorded
by modern botanists in P. Browne's 1756 work
titled *The Civil and Natural History of Jamaica*. In 1763, it
was classified by Jacquin as *Sicyos edulis* and by Adanson
as *Chocho edulis*. (You will note the origin of those surnames
and remember that a real and robust existence always, always
precedes classification.) In the most common variety, the fruit is
roughly pear-shaped, with a thin green skin coarsely wrinkled, fused
with the green to white flesh, and a single, large, flattened pit. The
flesh has a bland taste and a texture like a cross between a potato and
a cucumber. The chayote fruit is mostly used in cooked form. It is
usually handled like summer squash, lightly heated to retain its crispy
consistency. Like all fruits of the earth, including ourselves, chayote
is the subject of legends and myths, probably false. In Australia, where
it is called choko, people say that McDonald's apple pies are actually
made of chayotes, not apples. It is also believed that this fruit causes the
mummification of dead bodies in San Bernardo, Colombia, where it is
extensively eaten. Both fruit and seed are rich in amino acids and
vitamin C, the leaves and fruit have diuretic, cardiovascular, and
anti-inflammatory benefits, and a tea made from the leaves has
been used in the treatment of arteriosclerosis and hypertension
and to dissolve kidney stones, yet I once heard a TV chef
refer to chayote as "trash fruit." Strange how . . .
How strange that . . . but the truth,
like any shape we try to make,
is always, always strange.

ROASTED VEGGIES

When I peel the russet potatoes, the carrots, the sweet potatoes (and sometimes turnips), it's an occasion. When I cut the zucchini, asparagus, red peppers, it's an experience. When I bring out my largest bowl and use my hands to toss them all with olive oil, white wine vinegar, oregano, the trapdoor falls open, and I drop into a softness where tongue and nose are despots. The perfect music for this dark world happens only later: the dishwasher humming in the neat empty kitchen.

I had a roasted veggie dream last night, a frustration dream. No matter how I tried, I couldn't cut the veggies into the right shapes, and so no veggies were roasted. "The reason for your complaint lies, it seems to me, in the constraint your intellect imposes on your imagination" was what Schiller told someone who was having trouble writing. But no, it can happen from tiredness, or impoverished creative powers, or maybe something like what Emily Dickinson meant: "the mere sense of living is joy enough."

FOUND UNDER A CHAIR CUSHION

1. dark brown hair tie

One of a set, once primly wrapped around a card,
in varying shades of brown
meant to match the ponytail of
anyone who wanders into the CVS.

I don't know what color my hair is
so long have I paid to have it painted gold
as an October leaf
when the pavement is cool and wet.

2. *Mad Men* DVD
   Season 1, Disc 1

I tried to watch it, I really did.
It turned into an elephant, lumbering toward me.
Then it tiptoed like a Disney elephant, eyeing me
   coyly.
But lumbering and shillyshallying are
faddish. I wanted a bullet,
express and true,
I've always been a boy in that way.

The boys on the disc are splendid and shaved,
in white shirts, courtiers forming a circle
around the Sun King.
While the velvet folds of my spirit slept,
I believed I owed it to my generation
to act as a dutiful audience member.
In other words, even in the presence of the Sun
   King,
I tried being good but I got bored.

3. flyer for housecleaning service:
   Life's too short to clean your own home.

I agreed, and the family flew apart.
Couch flew apart, hand towels flew apart.
Dust overwhelms the lungs, twice daily.

Homer for example has never been out of print.
Is it because he lacked ambition for the clean life?
Capitalism + art + laziness, a dangerous formula!

4. seven dimes and one penny

Dimes are jewelry,
pretty beyond what monetary value
we endow them with.
With 71 cents I could buy
almost three-quarters
of a Snickers bar
but I'm off sugar.
71 cents is what I need
for three-and-a-half minutes
of garage parking on 12th Street
while I teach the willing and unwilling
how to laugh and cry
about line breaks.

Or the amount I earn
for every dollar earned by a man.

Or shall I adorn myself with coins
like a mad girl in tatters.

5. tweezer

It is time.
It is time to wrench out all the ugly hairs,
the Sun King approacheth!

6. redhaired Playskool® plastic kid
   dressed in jeans and gray hoodie,
   paint-spattered

This small person appears to be angry,
having spent ten years under a chair cushion,
having first suffered abuse
during some long-forgotten crafts project.
He is furious
but is nevertheless giving me
a thumbs-up.

OLD STRANGE BOOK

In the story of my life there is a field
filled with chicory, daisies, and mayflowers.
It's the field behind my childhood house.
In summer, I used to spend hours

lying in it looking at clouds
before my mother brought us to the town pool
where I spent some more hours swimming.
In the other seasons I went to school.

In the school there was a library.
In the story of my life there is a book.
The book was bound in rough green cloth.
Its glossy pages smelled oddly like puke.

The book told the story of two children,
Johnnie and Jill, I think.
They got lost in a deep forest,
drawn in thick dark ink.

They were brother-and-sister orphans.
They met fantastical creatures.
One was the goddess of spring,
or was that in Botticelli's picture

that I saw in the same library
in a book of art history for kids,
old European art of course.
The other kinds they did

not want us to know about.
The picture was magic
and so was *Johnnie and Jill*
though not a children's classic.

I don't really remember the title.
In the book the goddess of spring
rescues the children in trouble
and then—I can't remember a thing.

I'm sure there was a villain
in the book, probably a woman,
who practiced dark arts on a dark hill,
so evil she wasn't human.

In the story of my life there is a hill
that tamely rises above the field.
We sledded there in winter.
In spring our bikes wheeled

down the hill dangerously.
I walked on the hill this summer
tamely, carefully, slowly,
alongside my mother.

It isn't hard to say
what had brought us there.
We were old and middle-aged
in the knifelike summer air.

Slowly and tamely we walked
and I remembered the book.
It was called—*Julie and John*?
I wanted another look.

So what was the title?
And was it an allegory?
A Catholic one? (It was a Catholic school.)
That would ruin the story.

A story is only good if it's made up
but convinces you it's true.
Even better if one of the characters
is someone who could be you.

How else do you know who you are?
I once asked an old strange friend:
You only know you're the person who's with
the people you love, in the end.

From the hill I saw the house.
I imagined myself on the stair
clutching the wrought-iron rail,
a beanie on my bright hair.

On the hill I thought of the book.
That old strange book would save me.
But Google was not my friend
or maybe I was crazy.

Years had passed since I read
the book. My hair was darker,
my body had opened to make a person,
my cheekbones were starker.

Still I kept hold of the book
like a talisman or a bluff.
Any book I'd seen that was like it
was not like it enough.

Research didn't help
and memory is no good.
Longing was all I could do
and making up as much as I could.

Many books have I read, many people loved.
They mattered and mattered and mattered.
I tried but never found the book.
The field is where I'll be scattered.

YOUR ARDOR

To dream of your ardor
is much joy and much happiness.
Your ardor tells me that
I am making a mistake
by not taking hold of what
is offered to me.

What I mean when I say
"your ardor" is stenciled on
the air that surrounds
your big face. The force
of your ardor pushes strangely.

All that matters now
is your ardor. It solves
a most formidable equation.
How old is your ardor?
I think it was born when
it met me.

You should heed your ardor.
It will scoop you out, little melon:

  Your ardor as good as its master
  Your ardor tomorrow and your ardor yesterday
  Your ardor in January
  Your ardor dripping sharp as vinegar
  Your ardor dripping pale as ashes
  Your ardor with its quick reply
  Your ardor and your hot hard argument
  Your ardor with a hatchet
  Your ardor
  Your ardor drinking and talking
  Your ardor local and authentic
  Your ardor of lost fame
  Your ardor that hits the button and initiates
  Your ardor stronger than your pride
  Your ardor in squalor
  Your ardor that squeaks
  Your ardor that spends and spends

Your pen is my lure.
Your ardor my wire.

The night your ardor first beset me I cried
"Zyer! Oh, zyer!"
Who cares what I meant.
I don't retain facts.
We hate facts, don't we, they never did a thing for us.

Behind the screen of your ardor
lies the globe of the Earth
above which the eagle can be seen
soaring up toward the sun, which
has my face. It grins high in the purple sky.
On either side stand two allegorical figures,
the Way of Virtue and the Way of Vice.

Your ardor comes on like a pun,
making the most of
all possible significances.

Your ardor so close now to my ardor.
Our ardors twitch, so sensitive to control.
I just want your ardor to have fun in there!
What next, what next, oh ardors?

Here it is.
Here's what we call the *Red Spot*.

IRELAND

For two hours we sat on the plane and waited and a half.
Three. We took off. We flew over the dark.
You were a girl and we were flying. At home in Dublin
the first day and everyone and in the 70s and sunny.
The clouds rubbed on sea-light, "a real Irish summer."
Why two wolfhounds, two pigs, two swans?
How a dolphin for a shark? You gasped in alarm for the Cliffs
of Moher, the contraltos, selfies in the sweater you bought in Killarney.

Your Tumblr page; the handknotted sweater. The summer nearby.
We interpreted the swans and the dolphin, which you at first mistook.
Our hair frizzed in the chilly mist. I wondered how you would
stand me. We saw blossom and so were you. How unusual it was!
Our nips sharpened in the chill. Turf of our ancestors fortified
by the midnight pizza. The Atlantic fumed. You were fourteen,
how would you stand? Or how should contraltos sound in nearby summer
on our girls' journey that in the beginning the flight delayed?

TO THE POET WHO AFTER MY READING SAID "YOUR POEMS ARE GOOD. ECCENTRIC, BUT GOOD."

Imagine that you, at eighteen,
in Paris for the first time with
all your loving ideals about
penises intact, in your new
mini-trenchcoat and smelling the
smell of garlic and unfiltered
smoke and assaultive coffee, were
approached from behind. Imagine
un Français, bald smooth spectacled,
grabbed your right hand and pressed it to
his yes soft yes exposed penis
and hissed *"C'est chaud, hein?"* as he kept
walking past you shaking with his
poor French demented laughs. Would you
say "trauma" (it wasn't) would you
think "poem fodder" would you bring
to bear your rhetoric textbook
and wall of metaphors built up
from yes stone yes sky yes Shakespeare?

You no not arrogant mentioned
your encroaching baldness (which I
said that I yes liked). You were not
spectacled nor smooth but admire
I think smoothness? You didn't want
to say "bad" you couldn't commit
to good. Smoothly the current does
not run; smoothness can never shock.
When electricity veins through
the sky, is that really its *best*,
its crispest manifestation?
Must Emily Dickinson ride
through the yes "cloud-dark sky" on a
"flashing bolt" screaming "All men say
what to me"? Hands tattooed with the
small crosses that meant she couldn't

choose/settle on an *ideal* word?
Abandon possibility
fairer than prose for a what *word*?

Imagine this same hot lightning
snaking up your rectum. That was
childbirth 14 hours hard work!
And my husband's smell and my cow
moans and the doula's watered-down
grape juice helped. I couldn't call it
"pain" no "orgasm" no "earthquake"
closer but no. But I wanted
so to call it something. This is
the merry disease we share! I
suspected that the Queen's English
and I would not run smoothly then.
So I wept, past imagining.
Is it possible that death will
be a yes? Immortality
not a marble stone but a what
maxipad? A silver perfume?
There is no yes true metaphor.
Each eccentric as the others.

When I dab my wrists and neck with
the oily rollerball of my
favorite "perfume essence" (Rain
by TerraNova a bargain
at yes less than $20
for .3 oz. notes of lily
of the valley, clover, and musk)
I do it because it smells *fresh*,
like a *new earth*. Imagine that
same lightning struck you down on the
new earth dead. You'd say "critical
judgment" I'd say "poor social skills."
Imagine instead the lightning
struck the earth and a laurel bloomed
where once stood only tombstones! I
know it's hard to be a man, with
an ideal between your legs and

nothing but Shakespeare's cold lightning

waiting
              for you
                          on Judgment Day.

        Let's wait together.

We open our hearts and dictionaries.

You *were* waiting, weren't you,
for me to say "Gee, thanks"?
And are still what yes no waiting?

ATTITUDES AT THE NEW YEAR

1.

We get righteous.
In the presence of a hypothesis, any hypothesis, we get righteous.
Say a word: *immigrant*—and watch my father flinch, I boil,
you, maybe, cite data, someone else abandons the room.
Pieces of righteousness look like a river of baroque pearls with mean, red, pre-digital eyes.
We're barreling along and everything scarves a second
into a river of baroque pearls:

An image of 4000 friends, typing, all at each other's throats.
In January we enter the Hall of Dust, dressed in newness.
I wear the new cheeky spangles I've attached to myself.
Together they—pearls, spangles—make up a brilliant strand. But fake.
We all inhabit closets—beliefs—your own closet a time: 1987, 1991.
Now, while we dress up—smoky, sexy, vintage, the rest—
underneath we're warriors, angered, working in pajamas, from home.

Does the much-anticipated date remind you of a colored suit?
One you put on to protect yourself from ambiguity? We float far down the river,
far past those who waver or oppose. But what do we know?
I wear the best personal beliefs in high, high hand;
the debate pisses on, encasing the wretched in amber.
Am: a machine that confers final, urgent communications.
Must: clasp the poems that I put in golden jackets for the capsule.

So age I. So age my beliefs. Which does me in.

2.

Or ironic. When we hang on to the unexcitable, newest thing, a little suavely,
that particular three-quarter expression as pitiless as possible,
our true indifference drapes toward the world.
Look!: dinner at lunch: alcohol, pasta, cheese appear (we are fortunate)
with a triumph executed where? In the body, that concealer, that saint.
How bodies dart out between quips, reminding me, sometimes, to stop
the depressing nicks (of how many others?) in the "right" places.

That pale night when I looked to learn, really learn, the lesson of history,
just after the morning of the towers: Two old men traded wordplays,
well-meaning but so cut off. Their heads hurt, they hadn't slept.
As an antidote, I applied the usual pensive self-criticism,
but physical things—colors, shapes—had turned grumpy.
I saw, really saw, a stray face, a torso under a T-shirt, the elbow
that would go adamant in photographs.

There's an elegance in refusing the egregious, witty line.
As sleek as it is, it can alarm:
That pale night, I felt an array of many secrets, all being ignored,
until I saw and learned: the skin, the puniness of bodies,
frail under the arm, the breast, the armpit.
The body wears the light insisted by changes, it deserves an honest gaze
as it moves, at cruising speed, beyond the tired scorn.

Really? I thought. But it works.

3

Or infantile, which no one escapes. It starts on the sofa.
It's only the one rare afternoon, you think, when you have nothing to do,
you doze under a blankie, revisiting the house on Blue Creek Lane
where dozing began, revisiting your grandmother, her flat,
her loosely folded housedress. You recreate, always—what is the place called?
A certain kind of mindlessness, a certain failure to theorize,
a strange texture, like sweating, that annoys the highly strung.

This I chose for many years, out of weariness.
I find dull those tones called, heartbreakingly, professional;
I prefer heathered versions of the old freeplays in the leaf piles.
Cookies belong to youth but I order, always, the cookie platter,
a midsize bravado—the kind that was necessary
when adulthood sneezed like Satan from the linen shelves.
It is perhaps no longer efficient.

The leaf pile no swath of prairie, scenarios desperately real.
Yes, a giddiness remains, a small part devoted to mini-golf,
dreamfilled, feckless afternoons, magenta, aqua, yellow, all the colors of Florida!
But whimsy's a cheap solution. You resemble anything but the forgiving night
when you assert *I hate it! I love it!*, your work (*Just being exactly myself!*)
steered by how much *fun* it is, no guidance or plan, no care for ultimate effect.
The effusion must clear. You'll have to look forward, go forward,

gather your ragged power.

4.

The year ahead: a fortuneteller.
As soon as she comforts, she comes down to essentials,
 as wide as the spring, and as unimagined, and growing out, and up.
"Know," she says. "Help." More information please! Forward to what?
Try disdain, try letting go, try a child's approach? We have.
We've tried on attitudes like clothes, according to weather,
 only to find a sky full of clouds in unnameable heaps.

A catalogue of possible responses, is it really wholesome?
Why not just *act* when we hear "Help," surely a plea, not a command?
I long for inner multiples hitherto unknown,
 added layers, cut or thrown, a woman my age my size—but different,
 a few more, even a little preachy or dated, solidifying in the mirror at home.
One of them might know which attitudes (that once scratched but kept me warm)
 should be stored, in boxes, under the bed.

I fear a tragedy: acting, touching, but never enough,
 the whole year scorched, a curve of cotton fitted selfish to me.
It pulls, it snaps. The facts, sublime renegades, leave a mark.
If today we encounter a bizarre avatar of winter—unsuitable for cotton,
 muggy, violent, smelling like chains just broken—will it stay a long time?
A wavy sky, succulent mud, sky screaming, jays screaming?
But they never scream *ending*. I anticipate

the beginning with three promises: I begin. I'll act. I'm going to wait.

A VALLEY VIEW

To my left,
you, in the driver's seat.
Chlorophyll, to my right,

through the windowglass, green tipping
to black, tipping to gold, shivering.
Green hills, further on, shading

to blue. Fuzzed slopes, lovable, rolling down down.
Awkward weeds, sprigged, not wheat and won't feed anyone.
All is Dutch, set out for display and gain.

I've come to a conclusion about happiness: I want it.
You say "Sometimes you've got
to bust a move." How would I do that?

Through the windowglass I can get a fearsome burn.
Thus I'm SPF'd. I must earn.
On my lap, folderful of papers to which I should turn

but the sun does her thing: down down.
We don't see her cooling, but we gain
from her careful campaign.

Goodbye glimpse, speed past,
the green consummation tracks
everwards, lost—

Lost me, lost you,
lost green hills shading to blue
and lost the valley view . . .

ON BEAUTY

Firstly, you are beautiful,
moonfaced brothers and sisters.

But after that, what
is not open to question?

To pick up the torn wing
and paperclip it onto the angel

is a distortion rapidly done.
Distortion is beautiful,

and loud hearty laughter
as of the gods.

Beauty moves upward from the leaf,
downward from the root.

Beauty is quietly
born from boredom

into fabulousness or plainness.
Don't ask whether it exists.

It's a redundancy to say *real*.
Beauty is truth? Don't ask.

Ask for inner resources unlimited.
Ask for a goldfinch feather

in a balsawood box.
Look not at what is loved

but what stimulates and soothes.
Brothers and sisters,

are words beautiful or ugly
because we mean them

so very deeply?

A TRUE ACCOUNT OF TALKING
WITH A ROBIN ON THE MULCH,
NEAR MY RADIUS ORDAINED

What drama took place on the deck,
where I nursed a primitive state,
fear leading to anger!
With this, one July day
(my gray cat
sleeping beside me),
I avoided my poems
and the ways I could be of service.
The coming of fall,
the coming of fall—
I knew that my future was in loneliness,
in the hospital,
even in death.
Angst in the suburbs
is a despiséd thing.
I am a white middleclass woman
born in the 20th century,
enduring in the 21st,
who exists in herself,
answering her own ends,
who possesses
less than she wants
and more than she deserves.

On the deck I spoke out,
the words forced from me
by my ever-tyrannical
BIG FEELINGS,
"Why," I asked, "must it all
hasten so slowly?
Some story I tell,
with no pictures
and a bummer of an ending."
I shouldn't have expected an answer
but expectations linger,
just like memories.
No matter how much I had
that I didn't deserve,

I wanted more, more,
more adjustments to the universe
so that some approving eye
always turned, cheerily, toward me.
With a torpor worthy of a brown bear,
I didn't ask again,
but I couldn't resist a final statement,
aloud, to the uncaring
suburban summer regalia:
"Here am I," I whispered,
"oarless."

"It's a common confusion,
I have it myself,"
said a Robin, on the mulch,
full of wit and berries
(near my radius ordained).
Grateful for his attention
but unable to trust his wisdom,
I watched him, wary.
It was true. I observed
his utter whimsy and his
utter lack of conflict.
Trusting now, I began to speak
but before I could, he asked,
"What are you working on?"
as if he were chatting at
a literary cocktail party!
"Frankly, Robin, I'm stymied.
A novel, an essay, a couple of poems . . .
all stopped dead."
"*Hell* no!" he chirruped.
"You of all people know
that inspiration feels terrific
but isn't a great stockpiler.
And besides,
your ear, what an ear!
The world needs that.
Put all your future in it
and you'll have stars in your ink."

This bird, this glider, this chirruper,
whose *cheer up, cheerily*
woke me most mornings,
was a true friend!
I tried to be a friend to him:
"What brilliance!
Brilliance and beauty!"
At that moment,
a Mockingbird began screaming
at my gray cat,
my duststorm on the deck.
The cat had no wish
to attack the Mockingbird,
yet every morning
this screamer tormented him.
I was reminded of my anger.
I was angry at the Mockingbird
(though I knew the cat and I
are both natural predators)
and I was angry at aggression
wherever it occurs, and it occurred
everywhere that July.

The Robin saw.
"Breathe, dear! To a mother,
for example, as you well remember,
a tricycle can be more sinister
than a panther. And a wing
would be more eloquent
than that infernal screaming
but the poor thing doesn't know it.
Anger is only useful if it makes you fly.
You have to work to activate anger,"
he continued, cocking a sterner eye,
"work so that it enlivens
rather than oppresses, I mean,
but it's light work, not heavy."
I did breathe deeper then,
and I swear the cat relaxed too.
What a very small compass is salvation!
"Thank you, Robin!"

"It's time for me to go now,"
 the Robin asserted melodiously.
"I have my impulses to follow!
 Well, that, and I must feed myself.
 See that you do it too."
"Do *which* too?
 Follow my impulses or . . . ?"
 But I knew that the only answer,
 ever, is *Both*,
 and he knew I knew.
 Reluctant to let him go,
 I said, at the risk of seeming ungrateful,
"Robin, talking with you
 has been a marvelous refreshment,
 it reminds me of . . ."
"Vladimir and Frank, I know.
 Well?" "Well, I'm just saying . . .
 They had the Sun to talk to
 and I have you.
 And I wouldn't trade,
 believe me,
 but the Sun is large, universal, fiery,
 and full of majestic eruptions.
 While you're small, suburban,
 intermittent,
 and you modestly conceal
 your fiery breast
 under gray wings. Tell me,
 is it because I'm a woman?"

"I don't profess," he replied,
"to understand the ways of the muse.
 Certainly women's work of all kinds
 is shamefully undervalued.
 But consider,
 the Sun and I,
 we each wake sleepers.
 Some wake to light,
 some to song.
 Both seem equally charming
 from my perspective,

and I don't consider myself lesser.
I wake to light,
then I carry that light
through my song
to those still dreaming.
You're still dreaming."
With that, he flew,
the Mockingbird bowed
on his teetering branch,
and the day, the real day,
began.

JULY

July 1

Before Muriel goes to college,
we've decided to travel
north to south, continental:
14 states, 2 provinces, 18
days. She plans our route (MN to
FL), then I offer up my
Visa card. We need more. I borrow
against my 103B.
Someday she'll read & correct.

July 4

Independence is an outmoded
even dangerous concept
but the three of us go see
the fireworks on the river: the Chry-
santhemum, the Peony,
the one that fizzles like fresh
ginger ale. Our white independence
leaves dogs trembling under chairs
and other consequences.

July 8

Medium says: The Pain You Feel Is
Capitalism Dying
and Bernie calls Hillary
the "presumptive nominee." (I wish
I could correct this moment.
I was so sure it was the
right moment.) Mammogram this morning
and almost fainted from the
pain. I hadn't eaten break-

fast. The kind white technician pressed cold cloths
to my face and neck. Ashamed that I subjected her
to my drama.

I gave birth without ever wanting pain meds but the
mammo machine is a torture device. I'm not sure
why I'm supposed to get on board with having my
breasts injured every year (and being made to feel
like my breasts are just cancers waiting to happen).

Bloodletting and leeches.
Someday she'll read this
and laugh
and correct.

ON GIVING BIRTH

That night

I was

full of

information.

Her first word: More. Her first phrase: I need. Her first sentence: I need more.

July 10
New York to Minneapolis to Bemidji, MN

Plenty of emotion,
not much tranquility.
How many deaths
have I died on a plane.
Turbulence will never
knock a plane apart,
knock it from the sky.
With each jolt I call on
Jesus Christ by first and last
names and grab the hand
closest to mine, stranger
or (today) daughter.

She corrects: A plane is a physical object in an imperfect world. You expect bumps.

I am a physical coward and I am an introvert.
I also do not easily believe that anyone is interested in my thoughts, presence, or opinions.

After what happened in Dallas and in Baton Rouge,
I ~~can't abdicate can't bring~~ can't feel right bringing Muri
who breathes because of:

a placenta I made
blood I brewed
body I formed
spirit I've been gentle with
(Shame: *tried* to be gentle with)

spirit I tried to be gentle with

into a possibly violent Black Lives Matter protest.
I abdicate our original plan.

We decide instead (snobs)
to have a cultural experience
while we still can.

Minneapolis Institute of
Art: a special exhibit
of landscape paintings. On the
wall an Edward Hopper quote: "My aim
in painting has always been
the most exact transcription

possible of my most intimate
impressions of nature." We
see Hockney's Grand Canyon, a
misinterpreted O'Keeffe ("canyon"
that is really a cunt), and
Venice by Turner et al.

"Enough with the Venice!" Muri stops
at an ornate papal ink-
stand (about the size of a
microwave oven). "Come off it!" she
tells the patriarchy. She likes best
the room filled with Frank Lloyd Wright

models and furniture. "You like ob-
jects." "Yeah, I don't like art. I
mean, I don't not like it but
I don't need to think about it like
you do." I notice a white
man staring at her breasts (which

are gorgeous, to be fair) and have the
impulse to strangle him. Pro-
tectiveness or jealousy or both?

Earlier, in the Enterprise car
rental office, a gorgeous
clerk alone at the counter
with 7 people waiting on line.
Suddenly she let out a
loud burp and a gagging sound

then ran to the back where we supposed
there was a restroom. After
several minutes, I went
and knocked on the door. "I just
wanted to see if you were
OK. Are you OK?" She

came out, looking ill. She gave me a
weak smile and a look that said
"No. No, not really OK."

On our way to Bemidji,
where we'll spend the night,
re her 18th birthday
at college:
"If I don't
have friends,
I'll get
a tattoo."

"All my friends are atheists." "It's a
construct," I say. She knows all
about my Catholic child-
hood, how I'm not religious now but
I can't escape the early
imprinting and believe—know,

really—that a universal force
exists with no outside of
it. Which because of early
imprinting I call God. "People my
age don't need it anymore."
We look out at the two-lane

road, birch and pine and blacktop far as
we can see. "Unless you lived
out here. You'd need the drama?"

ABORTION KILLS 4000 AMERICANS A DAY
(about as many "friends" as I have on Facebook)

44

Now, in the hotel room:

The gorgeous clerk in the Enterprise office was Black

was maybe pregnant

(which does and doesn't matter)

(which is worth writing and not worth writing).

1000 protesters have shut down I-94, the same highway we drove from Minneapolis on.

Weekend of Rallies, Demonstrations, Protests. A Children's March.

And a Musicians' Protest for Peace in front of the capital.

The very young white spiky-haired blond anchor says "Now that's the kind of protest we want to see."

White police chief says of the protesters: "I was disgusted by the behavior of some. Not all, some."

There is no outside of this. Onscreen
a Black woman holding a
sign at one of the protests,
the sole indisputable truth/lie:
NOT ONE MORE. And I was more
stirred than I am by great art.

July 11
Bemidji to Angle Inlet to Roseau, MN

We walked a little way around the lake
on a new path,
planned but pleasant.

Walked out on a pier. Unfamiliar
wildflowers: a fuchsia bell
on a silver leafless stalk
like the fairy wand now laid away
in the dress-up trunk at home.
   Then: Photo in front of the
concrete statue of Paul Bunyan and
Babe the Blue Ox. Back in St.
Ambrose School, I wanted to
connect with that tall tale but instead
I felt two obstacles: Paul
was a boy, his clothes dreary.
Old folk songs Polly Wolly Doodle
Oh Susanna Jimmy Crack
Corn: I brought her up on them

but I'm a perpetual immigrant in my mind, an impostor.

It's easy to love a country if you avoid its people.

To get to Angle Inlet, the true northernmost part of our journey, we drive through woods coniferous, mostly sky. We have to cross into Canada for about four miles, then cross back into the US.

The smiling white Canadian border agent: "Hello, ladies. What brings you to Canada today?" We outline our quixotic purpose. "OK, gals, have a great time!"

He explains that we have to call in to US customs when we get to "Jim's Corner,"

then proceed to Angle Inlet

then call in to Canadian customs on our return. "We're the only two nations in the world that allow customs by phone. US and Mexico don't do that!"

he says proudly.

Jim's Corner: I'd pictured a sort of general store, where the call to customs would be made homespun by donuts and interesting hardware. And Jim.

Instead, a muddy corner lot with a rotary phone handset. When we get out of the car, we're targeted by flying insects as conscious as birds. On our way, we'd seen birds "like ravens who've been working out at the gym."

Angle Inlet: A flock of white pelicans loiter wearily in the water near the shore. A caretaker, a white man, drives up in a truck and throws them some fish. Immediate frenzy: displays of aggression, slapping wings, expansion of their sullen mouth-pouches.

The drawing of a pelican in my mother's prayerbook, pricking her own breast with her long pointed beak so that her starving babies could drink her blood. A symbol of Jesus who shed his blood to save us

& O the maternal martyrdom.

OED app tells me John Skelton wrote:

Then sayd the Pellycan:
When my Byrdts be slayne
With my bloude I them revyve.
Scripture doth record
The same dyd our Lord
And rose from deth to lyve.

We're staying the night in Roseau:

Don't tread on me flag.
        Huskie trotting along side of road.
                "Oh well can't see everything."

CLEANSING WAVE GOSPEL CHURCH
JESUS REALLY LOVES US

I'D RATHER BE A CONSERVATIVE NUTJOB THAN A LIBERAL
WITH NO NUTS AND NO JOB

(bumpersticker on pelican feeder's truck)

July 12
Fargo, ND

"Bagels" aren't enough.
"Salads" aren't enough.

In a hipster hotel, we eat "real" food for the first time in 3 days.

A summer berry salad with cheddar shavings. 3 big scallops in red Thai curry.

lyric interlude: the world has eaten me it's proven untrue
the world is eating me it doesn't know better
the world will eat her and now I must shed her

Bernie endorsed Hillary today.

And the funeral for 5 police officers in Dallas.

She always frays when she gets too hungry and we ate a late small breakfast and skipped lunch. By five o'clock she was frantic and too hungry to eat and she wouldn't say yes to the Falls Overlook Café although we were right there. She found on her phone an expensive restaurant downtown. I lost it and shouted that it'd be a half hour before we got there, sat down, ordered, and got food there.

(Shame:

> She'd been nursing—
> "like a champ" said the doula—
> from her first moments in the
> world. When they turned out the
> lights in my room, I allowed a
> nurse to take her to the nursery
> ("baby kennel," Rob said). An
> hour later the nurse came back
> and woke me up. "Your baby's
> crying. Do you want to feed her?"
> "No, give her a bottle.")

The sun had been in my eyes all day, stinging them even behind sunglasses, along with the melting sunscreen, and by eight o'clock it was still aggressive as noon. I felt attacked, wanted to attack the nearest vulnerable thing.

GUNS GOLD AND ROCK N ROLL

A Corvette convention in town, the downtown streets closed off and lined with Corvettes. The owners strolled past and sat at outdoor tables drinking beer (the guys) and wine (the wives). They're mostly in their 60s, white, prosperous-looking in an unpleasant way. Prosperity that has abdicated responsibility. Smug, was my interpretation. Their phallic substitutes looked cute and slightly threatening, as if they might spurt any minute.

Still I wouldn't mind a ride in a Corvette.

                                   Enjoyed the highest speed limit so far today,

                      80 mph. I pushed to 90, the distances so distant and the

road there so flat and foreshortened.

We saw colts but
Muri called them
ponies. Didn't
I teach her the
difference when
she was seven?
What else haven't
I taught her?

In Falls Park, we watched a mother duck and a duckling get what seemed to us too
close to the edge of the falls. The water rushed furiously around them and it seemed
impossible that the duckling wouldn't be swept over. The mother was unconcerned,
turning away from the duckling, often diving into the water for plants or fish. The baby
was so tiny. But held its own and made its way into a little hollow in the rocks, and the
mother followed.

We moved to sit in the cool grass in the shade of an evergreen with long lethal needles.
Then a police car drove into the parking lot not far from where we were sitting. Muri
clutched my hand. "One of them's getting out his gun." I couldn't see (sun in eyes) and I
couldn't honestly tell her the fear was irrational.

"Where are they going?"
"They're talking to a man who's sitting on the path. He's naked.

                                                          Let's go."

July 14
Loess Hills State Forest, IA

Attack in Nice, where I spent a year
in college. A truck plowed in-
to a square where a crowd was
celebrating Bastille Day. More than
100 dead. ISIS claims
responsibility but

ABSTRACT	LOCAL	COMMERCE
love and trust	lethal pine needles	Booze Bros
call and response	distance so far	Touchless Car Wash
duty and pleasure	smell of clove disinfectant-dogs-cows-prairie in the pet exercise area of the rest stop	Car Wash Liquor Available

DRIVING

Sign for twisty road like ouroboros unlocked

POLITICAL POEM

COOL STORY BABE, NOW SHUT UP AND MAKE ME A SANDWICH
Take a mental picture

Keep Calm and Carry
I love Canadian Boobies

Crowns are always in style!
#smile

Save the Hooters—Breast Cancer Awareness
Pugs Not Drugs

In dog beers, I've only had one
Respect all Fear none

Like a BOSS
God Only Knows

Goal Driven
This is the part where I nod and act like I'm listening

Pardon my French
Thank God I'm Fresh

Don't laugh: it's YOUR girlfriend's shirt
Ain't nobody got time for dat

Daddy's Little Hoosier
Just a Texas girl in a Georgia world

Er mah gerd
Trying to get star spangled hammered

I don't get drunk, I get awesome
Got Freedom?

Collect and destroy
Go fuck your #selfie

Today: Hike in the Loess Hills (pronounced *LUSS*) (not lust not loss).

Curving yellow path through the crisp-dry green grass. View like *The Sound of Music* which we sing in cheesy opera voices.

Girl with dark ponytail on the trail striding ahead of me into her future. Hello.

I give her dominion

Over the yellow-orange moth I give her dominion

Over the thistle I give her dominion

Over the hills I give her dominion

Over the armies of men I give her dominion

Because she is gentle I give her dominion

July 15
Kansas City, Independence, Lee's Summit, Branson, MO

Time is a river until it's a wall. Time a river until it's a plot.

We pick Rob up at the Kansas City airport. Immediately the atmosphere changes: Three.
Plus testosterone.

We go to the Truman Library. Reactions pro and con to Hiroshima, on a wall.
More testosterone.

Worth writing and not worth writing:

Lee's Summit, my gaze:

A Black man walking through a small park,
among the geraniums,
unconcerned, checking his phone

                    Two Black families in the condo complex in Branson

                              Black kids in the gameroom

surprise and hearten me.

My gaze doesn't ask: Who am I heartening?

To get to Branson we drive by a lake with the tops of leafless trees growing
up from it as if after a nuclear holocaust.

Political ads on TV in the condo:

He's not who you think he is. He's just another liberal.
I support life and religious freedom.
I'm not a politician, I'm a constitutional lawyer.

When Muri says something's going on with Turkey we think she means a buffet in
Branson.

Song on radio in car: *City life never meant that much to me.*

But I said I could only live in a place if I could walk to a café.

How long ago did Michael Brown die?
He was a Missourian
until time became a wall,
a plot.
Heartening me, saddening
me is 20th c. at

                                        best. But how to subtract myself?

MISSOURI

You don't know how to live with unkindness
but you are not tied to a tree.
You say: We all need a safe lake.
A lonesome day.

No not dancing only playing.
No not killing only playing.
Who leapt about with strange cries?
Who smoked kicked and partied?

And would sass to the last.
A defiant day.
A delirium, really.
Repeat: It's not about you IT'S NOT ABOUT YOU.

*

Repeat: It's not about you IT'S NOT ABOUT YOU.
In Huck Finn's country,
who sassed, oh who sassed
and who sassed and sassed?

We saw melodies in the trees.
We smelled an immensity, yum.
We are a melting quilt, with yardfire.
The safe lake, collected tears, all gulped up.

History rolls onto you while you sleep
but you don't know until nine months later.
Will
never be safe and you will neither.

July 16
Branson, MO

I wake up to Rob's salty smell. And
the fucking sun.   Replica
of Empire State Building topped
by King Kong. At first I think it's the
World Trade Center tower with
its plume of smoke.   Replica

of *Titanic*. We're each given a
passenger's name and have to
wait until the end of the
tour to find out whether we survive.
I survive. Muri survives.
Rob, as a male crew member,

doesn't survive.   Toy Museum: quotes
from Bible on walls. BB
gun annex. Segregated
cabinets with Black Sambo and Aunt
Jemima dolls. Careless piles:
dusty board games, unloved dolls.

What I thought I had learned about towns: Where there is money, towns are pleasant
and where there is no money, towns are unpleasant.

But there has to be a quietness too.

We play mini-golf, our family sport, at Pirate's Cove.

MINI-GOLF

The object of the game is to be a family sport. The object of a family is to self-destruct.

Mini-golf, like a family, creates its own artificial world.

Mini-golf, like a family, trades in myths and legends.

In both, there are markers of individuality (club heights, ball colors) (contradiction, rebellion, separation).

Both are at their most intense in summer.

Money troubles tend to disrupt each. The mini-golf boom of the early 20th century came to an end during the economic depression in the late 1930s.

Mini-golf and families are for those who wish the past different.

Mini-golf was invented in the United States, as was my family.

The object of the United States is to self-destruct. Can I prevent it with my pink putter and orange ball, driving into the artificial sandtrap, or farther,

far into the myth of the unblemished (bloody) summer?

Very late, Rob and Muri asleep. I watch Harold Bloom talking about the canon and Jesus on YouTube.

He quotes Huey Long: *Of course we will have fascism in America but we will call it democracy.*

In the south and southwest, HB found, people have conversations with Jesus on daily basis. *He knew and loved them intimately.*

Best *African American* poets are Jay Wright, Robert Hayden, Thylias Moss, but all are *too dense and difficult for the Afro-American-centrists to bother with.*

I think we are in a very bad way indeed.

I want to read a biography of Harold Bloom's mother, Donald Trump's mother, Bob Dylan's mother.

Spend a day in Branson, MO, and I run to Harold Bloom as to a cool fountain.

July 17
Branson, MO to Memphis, TN

Rob drives and I sleep most of the way.

"You just slept through the cutest town." Covered sidewalk.

Biscuits and jam in diner in small-town TN. I pick up a free Chick tract from a basket by the door.

> HEART
> TROUBLE?
> "There's ugly
> things down deep
> in your heart that
> we can't see
> . . . But God
> does."
>
> *The heart is deceitful*
> *above all things and*
> *desperately wicked:*
> *who can know it?*
> Jer. 17:9

Sun Studio tour. Photo of Rob at the mike where Elvis Presley sang "Mystery Train."

Soul food at Miss Polly's on Beale Street: second good meal we've had.

July 18
Memphis, TN to Florence, AL

The ducks in the Peabody lobby
Parade on schedule only.

We walk along the Mississippi where the Trail of Tears began.

95 degrees. We mist ourselves in the kids' misting park.

Drive Rob to the airport. He has to get back to work. Goodbye.

Rob who, in a phrase from a Robyn Selman poem, "funds our insolence."

Drive to Florence, AL, where Helen Keller was born. Suddenly everyone seems educated and prosperous; the hotel breakfast offers do-it-yourself ambrosia with blackberries and grapefruit segments and slivers of pineapple and shreds of coconut and toasted almonds for sprinkling.

Where there is money, towns are pleasant.

On our way we stop at a grocery store in a town where I see (I feel pretty sure) the poorest people I've ever encountered besides urban homeless people. Unlike urban homeless people, they do not ask for my help.

We buy cashews (misshapen and non-cashew-tasting) and blueberries (good).

The clerk, a white woman of around 70, with gray hair in pincurls, a thin pink polyester smock, wire glasses, uses an oldfashioned mechanical cash register.

She fumbles making change and I, asshole, can't just patiently wait but tell her how much it should be. I do it smilingly, questioningly, I'm a nice asshole.

Watched Republican convention in Cleveland. Retired General Michael Flynn's speech:

determined American who loves our country   (scared little boy)
wake up America
no substitute for American exceptionalism   (afraid he doesn't
                                                    exist)

Americans should not fear our enemies
USA yer darn right   (mother washed his
                                                    mouth out with soap)

Get fired up (in robot voice)   (father whipped him
                                                    for crying)

We know
We know
that America is the greatest country in the history of the world
Let there never be a substitute for American exceptionalism
It must never fade   (Wearing his ancient
                                                    hurts and rages like a
                                                    flak suit)

Trump Trump there ya go
Unrelenting goal
reckless rhetoric
Obama clone

with conviction in our beliefs   (his voice breaks)

pierces through

fearlessness n courage   (hurt_n_rage.com)

Americans stand as one
new American century   (commodity)
relentless focus

protect our families
with our feet firmly planted on the ground
holding individuals accountable
our new American century   (buy now)

political correctness and senseless hyperbole

USA USA you got it you got it   (in robot voice)
that's right that's right

USA USA USA   (in robot voice)

I mean God help us
Get fired up
I love it

To vote is to admit that you don't take up as much space as you'd like to imagine.
I wish I could vote for a tree.

July 19
Caney Creek Falls, AL; Birmingham, AL

Yes, trees are magic.
Yes, cities are magic.
Yes, I eat the magic and spit out the seeds.
Yes, I am a machine.
I am a machine that makes waste.
I am a sorting machine.
I am a white sorting machine.
I am a white middleclass female sorting machine,
sorted.
I am a sorting machine that likes soft and pleasant things.
I am a sorting machine that buys soft and pleasant things.

Hike to Caney Creek Falls. We park at
the top of an old logging
road and descend. Muscadines
and blackberries line the trail. The falls
drop from a rocky cliff,
which forms a sort of amphi-
theater. We stand under: cool bliss.
All our sunscreen washes off.
I carefully reapply
mine to protect my pale, sallow skin.
Muri has Rob's beautiful
tanned Mediterranean
skin, so not so important for her.
Only cigarette butts and
disposable diapers tell

us we aren't the discoverers.

Civil Rights Institute in Birmingham, across the street from the 16th Street Baptist
Church, bombed in 1963, where the 4 girls

Addie Mae Collins, Denise McNair, Carole Robertson and Cynthia Wesley

were killed. Still there, shining and repaired.

A churchly place. Point to a random building in a southern city: it has a better chance of
being a church than anything else. The names are a poem:

Abyssinia Missionary Baptist
East Lake Full Gospel Baptist
Ebenezer Baptist Church
Evergreen Missionary Baptist
Green Liberty Baptist Church
Galilee Baptist Church
Groveland Baptist Church
Harmony Street Baptist Church
Lilly Grove Baptist Church
Mount Calvary
Mount Carmel
Mount Moriah
Mount Olive
Mount Zion
New Hope Baptist Church
True Life Missionary Baptist
Gloryland Baptist Church
The Greater Works Baptist Church
Upper Room Baptist Church
Restoring the Kingdom Ministry
Vestavia Church of Christ
St. George the Great Martyr (Melkite)
St. Elias Maronite Church
All Nations Deliverance Center
Shepherd of the Hills
Christ Temple Deliverance
Fullness Christian Fellowship
Integrity Bible Church
More Than Conquerors Faith
New Lines Ministry
Walking on Water Christian Church
Warriors of the Word Christian

My father had a Louis Armstrong album when I was little. The cover was an extreme black-and-white closeup of Louis's face, on a blue-black background, shining with sweat, eyes closed. I thought he was Jesus. How else would he look so sufficient, transported?

I said to Muri
(she'd planned too much driving today):
"You're expecting too much of me."

Had to go to an Apple store to buy a charger for my antique MacBook. I'd left mine in the Memphis hotel and I needed to finish teaching my online class. Glossy mall outside of Birmingham: The Summit.

J. Crew
Lilly Pulitzer
Coach
Macaroni Grill
Banana Republic
Brow Art 23
Anthropologie
Lucky Brand Jeans
Bravo! Cucina Italiana
free people
Aveda
Pottery Barn Kids
Kopper Popper
Motherhood Maternity
bebe
Sur La Table
Madewell
Scentology
Teavana
Michael Kors
Victoria's Secret
Kendra Scott
Vera Bradley
kate spade new york
J.Jill
Trader Joe's
francesca's
Brookstone
Journeys
Justice

Also a poem.

We saw a Black mother and teen daughter: like white me and Muri but ten times better dressed, coiffed, and made up. Also much much cleaner.

I've been watching YouTube makeup tutorials at night in the hotel rooms.

Hampton Inn on the Alabama-Georgia border. Our phones keep toggling between Central and Eastern time.

July 20
Columbus, GA

Whitewater rafting on Chattahoochee River. Our guide Eric; his river name ("everyone has one") is Gypsy.

We ride with a woman in her 40s who's with her 15-year-old son (mildly autistic) and his mostly silent friend. It's her birthday and this is on her bucket list. When Gypsy calls her "mama bear" once I think maybe it's endearing or meant to be, a southern thing. When he does it repeatedly I think

(1) hey, I'm a mama too

(2) an overly familiar, dehumanizing reference to her skin color?

(3) mamas pressed together in a raft. We scream at the same time but apart.

Trump is everywhere, on every screen. I do a meditation exercise. I try not to hate him. The only way I can do it is to see him as a troubled child who needs to be restrained and retrained.

Rafting lingo:

hot tub: sitting on floor of raft when going over rough rapids, holding tight to upright paddle (but I lose mine anyway when it gets stuck between two rocks).

floating: slipping out of raft into the river and hanging on while we glide downstream. One by one, Gypsy hauls us back in as we approach the next rapids.

July 21
Panama City, FL

The latest shooting in North Miami, where we'll be in a few days: Black caretaker of a
Black autistic man, lying on street next to him with hands raised,

                                                        shot in the leg by a Latino cop.

"I thought he wouldn't shoot me if I was on the ground with my hands raised. Wow, was
I wrong."

Video:

"Why'd you shoot me?"   "I don't know."

Trump gave his acceptance speech tonight,
introduced by Ivanka.
Years ago he said if she
weren't his daughter he'd date her, and
I understood why Dante
had to write his *Inferno*.

LIFEWAY MINISTRY: YOU'RE WORTH IT.

Sunset boat ride: We watch dolphins leap
modestly out of the bay
to inhale-exhale. We stand
at the ship's front rail, "I'm king of the
world"-style. Muri sees a cute
guy, edges away from me.

Later the sky turned an electrified coral-lavender, with big crazed horizontal shards of lightning splitting it.

I had a flash of the old woman I'll be someday: a little elegant, a little dotty, a little inward, a little quick to touch people's hands.

A saint is someone who absorbs hatred and doesn't pass it on.

gators melons gator jerky hot boiled peanuts T-shirts

July 22
Panama City to Orlando, FL

I woke up hyper-aware of the
visual impression I
make on the world. I am not
beautiful. I'm not even ugly
or strange-looking. Small breasts, wide
hips: my physical person

is quite negligible.   McDonald's
between Panama City
and Orlando: a rawfaced
bossy white woman in her 40s
swaggered over to the Black
studious-looking teenage

cashier. Her (white woman's) boxy white
T-shirt: DON'T JUDGE US. But I
do.   Hillary preceded
us in Orlando by a few hours.
Brought white roses to Pulse night-
club, site of shooting last month.

Before we went rafting yesterday, I
took off my necklaces (gold chain with pendant
of Raphael's cherub that my grandmother
brought me from Italy when I was 10,
diamond that A. left me) and put them . . .
where? I thought in a pocket of
suitcase, tote, or handbag. I delayed
looking for them because I knew I'd
be an emotional shitshow if I couldn't
find them. Looked this morning. Couldn't find.
Emotional shitshow: I threw myself
on the bed and wept. Not really just
about the necklaces. The art of losing
is mastering me. Muri calmly tried
to talk some sense: "Let's make a plan." We looked
systematically in every pocket
of every bag. Finally I found them stuffed
in one of my balled pairs of socks. WTF?

"Was it the angel you were really worried about?"

"No, they're both talismans."

Jesus is still the answer.

To pass the time on the six-hour drive we take BuzzFeed quizzes:

What kind of diva are you? (Me: Beyoncé, Muri: Adele)
What classic rock group are you? (Me: Rolling Stones, Muri: Pink Floyd)
What Broadway musical should you see? (Me: *She Loves Me*, Muri: *Fiddler on the Roof*)

Lonely confused angry depressed? Jesus is still the answer.
Real men love babies: Heartbeat 18 days.

July 23
Orlando, FL

Disney World: Faces of two-year-olds
waiting on line for more than
two hours for a 10-minute
"attraction" look like the faces of
the damned. No redemption or
reprieve: it's God (their parents)
doing this to them. Old age looms and
with it, Last Times. Is this the
Last Time I'll be at Disney

World? Hope so. By the end of our 12
hours (heat 100 degrees,
two rides we'd looked forward to
closed, shame of being there at all), I
feel defeated by Disney.
Then the urge to go back and
do it again "right." I'd use the My
Disney Experience app,
for one thing.

                    I did enjoy:

frozen lemonade
in a little pocket garden a perfect green lizard only half an inch long
sushi at Epcot
virtual reality ride where you feel like you're flying over the Sahara, Taj Mahal, Alps,
Egyptian pyramid, Eiffel Tower

Shooting today in Munich and bombing in Kabul.

July 24
Orlando to Miami, FL

Didactic doggerel, directed at myself only, as penance for Disney:

ON THE FLOOR WITH A BLANKET OVER MY HEAD, TOWARD A SYSTEM OF VALUES

We all need a safe lake.
Safety is something to give, not take.

I have some work to do.
I means me, not you.

A day with no new news.
Stop listening for the muse.

It's simple politeness:
Listen to the people who live in your mess.

I hereby abdicate
my power. Too late.

I won't eat men like air.
That would not be fair.

I am Huck Finn. At most.
Shut up and listen. Don't boast.

All right then, I'll go to hell.
The very words are like a bell.

Safety is something to give, not take.
We all need a safe lake.*

---

* This line, repeated twice in this sad excuse for a poem (and also used in an earlier entry), appeared originally
in a poem written by a classmate in a workshop taught by Rob Fitterman, the first poetry workshop I ever took,
at the West Side Y on 63rd Street. I wish I could remember her name.

On the highway, two Latina girls in the back of a pickup truck, eating a snack, their long hair excited in the breeze.

At last, white powder beach and the friendly Atlantic. We wade in.

Posh (white) town with a mask of slackerdom. Someone made the money. Who and how?

Bernie addressing the DNC now.

Muri says they all sound so fake.

I'm reading books of poetry like they're clementines and I have scurvy: Spahr Buffam Schiff Mayer. White women.

There's whiskey in the jar
Confederate flag on the car

Roosters strutting around Old Town remind me of Elizabeth Bishop's war poem. (white woman)

Walked to Southernmost Point. Waves slapped the embankment and we slapped the concrete buoy monument. Made it.

"We've produced by far the most progressive platform in the history of the Democratic Party," says Bernie. "I am proud to stand with her."

ON GENDER

I said to Muri over key lime pie
that we need more feminine energy
in power, to challenge the patriarchy.

(Feminine meant Bernie.) She disagreed:
she doesn't think any-
thing is gendered. I modified:

Nurturing energy
instead of dominating energy.
Then she could agree.

Are mothers always a mystery
to daughters? I don't want to be.

July 26
Key West, FL

Last night (the convention) I was so dispirited that I wanted to open the bottle of Two-Buck Chuck the Miami Airbnb host left and drink myself to sleep. Today I'm more resigned and because we have to move on into the future, I have hope.

Muri in pain from her period today. We did next to nothing: late brunch and visit to Hemingway's house. Highlight: the six-toed cats, of course.

Dropped Muri off at our room then walked to Elizabeth Bishop's house.

ON MEMORY (ON POETRY?)

> I remember it
> (from 2000) as
> a white house with a
> very high white fence
> around it. Either
> someone took down the
> fence or else I'm mis-
> remembering. Or
> maybe she had two
> addresses in Key
> West? And my poem
> about the house with
> the sign about dog
> sweaters* may be a
> complete figment too.
> No sign except for
> one next to the front
> door that said HIPPIES
> USE BACKDOOR and a
> formal plaque on the
> gate (first I typed fate).

*"Aquí se puede comprar camisetas perro"
from *The Search Engine*

In the noiseless siesta streets: lots of meaty succulents, lots of scattered stone.

I remember a story I heard about Elizabeth Bishop and her lover Louise Crane, how they bought a house together in Key West and then Louise went back to New York and Elizabeth wrote "Letter to N.Y." for her ("In your next letter I wish you'd say / where you are going and what you are doing") and then Elizabeth surprised Louise by paying a visit and was in turn surprised to find Louise in bed with "a musician friend" (when Elizabeth told the story afterwards she named Billie Holiday). Then I remember her poem with the bad title ("The time has come to call a halt; / and so it ends"). Then I remember how tired I am of sleeping alone.

Muri and I talked about how to deal with her period at college. Like me, she has 24 bad hours a month. She said she'll just go to her classes and spend the rest of the 24 hours in bed. I tell her about cultures that have separate huts where menstruating women can be outside of their daily lives, be taken care of by the other women. Some also stay in bed, swaddled along with their newborns, for a month after they give birth. That always sounded right to me.

Later we go out for ice cream, sweat
sluicing our backs. I ask for
chocolate amaretto
in a cone. The depressed-looking man-
ager, a white guy around
60, says "The flavors with

alcohol are too soft for cones. I'm
sure you know that alcohol
doesn't freeze." A futile bit
of information. "No, I didn't
know but OK . . ." He looks at
me blankly and offers to

accommodate: ice cream in
a cup with cone stuck on top.

ISIS knife attack in a church in France
shooting at a teen club in Fort Myers
shooting in Munich

MOTHERHOOD

A pineapple is grandma to a porcupine.
A candle is grandma to a pair of wax lips.
Each thing gives birth to something more vivid than itself
and so on.

Stopped at a Starbucks on the way to the airport. Yes, corporate devil but it's that or
Waffle House . . . had to make a U-turn.

Gospel song on radio: Jesus is with me when I need him most.

YOU ARE LEAVING Key West   Paradise USA

Nothing feels like what it's supposed to feel like.

THE PERFECT DAY

Every
penetrating
warm

I
that
is
is
thrilled

Uproarious
august
other

Un-
commercial
splashing

Fizz-water
wet
and
spilled
on
me

The
cloud
heap

and
we
can
like
the
swell

My advice, dear one: Don't expect to get through life holding on to beliefs. Let new ones wash over you like the friendly Atlantic. Let new beliefs fall on you like rain from the sky.

Dreading in a way going home but also so ready. I want to wash all my white cottons.

Our flight delayed. We get in so late I don't want to make Rob pick us up. *We'll Uber home.*

Very late: Uber home with guilt: How can it be so cheap?

THE
GODDESS

ON HOPE

How do we get in? Opens a door
through which we can, impulsively, pop?
We need faith while the possible is possible.
After, we need hope.

Just as we need a mother,
or an angel, an everlastingly kind ungendered being.
The astronomer drops to the floor a key
to prove a universe of bodies all attracting each other.

The key falls. But if attraction,
how then does the floor not rise to meet the key?
The question stays green wherever we seed it. The key falls
and the floor does rise infinitesimally to meet it.

THE GODDESS

1. {The election; Muri cries; I decide to read Paradiso *as antidote}*

The moon was very halved. The girl on the phone sobbed
I didn't think it could happen. All nature and human nature
seemed halved in one quick night. She had canvassed and canvassed,
a behavior we believed artistic. The hammered throng mobbed
the hotel ballroom, glared and danced: picture
of an evil species, bareassed.
And sloppy greed for the easy fix, the dumbest.

And I too dumb to see a fix. The future lost its color.
When Dante climbed away from the vile circles,
he swapped saints for criminals
and the lines pushed onward, duller.

Dull or not, I craved rigor. I crowdsourced a translation.
I found dull *Paradiso* online and clicked on one iteration.

2. {I look up two words; Beatrice points out the immorality of optimism}

Reading *Paradiso*, I couldn't remember
what *fascist* and *demagogue* precisely meant.
I kept looking them up: *A person*
who is extremely right-wing or authoritarian.
A political leader who seeks support by appealing to prejudice, not logic.
That way, it turned out, many of us leant.
Optimism was blindered, immoral. Therefore we had greatest need of it.

Sure it's an artwork but we needed a prayer.
Dante read the world of people as a book of morals
and the solar system as a concert en plein air
and Paradise a stage with lighting favorable.

You, optimist, have been—ahem—less than serious!
said the know-it-all bitch of Paradise, Beatrice.

3. {Anatomy of optimism}

I was no know-it-all: I had hope.
Reading *Paradiso* I hoped *our* story could end happily
even if our every screen talked differently.
Underneath the latest haircuts, you could recognize
the befuddled faces, the scared eyes
halfway up the icy hell-slope.
All said: *Just wait. Death will seep in—*

death is no apocalypse, except by projection.
Don't let the bombs hear! I cried, fearing fear could self-fulfill.
But the unguessed-at can always happen.
Our guesses alone won't fill the bowl.

History is junk: There's no way to get the story whole.
Ice has only one direction: forward and fall.

4. {I wonder about happiness}

Reading *Paradiso*, I couldn't remember
what I thought happiness was. A tradeoff for knowledge?
Resonance of form and vibration of color?
The compulsive writing of sonnets?
A docent in the museum of memories? The long-
worked-for achievement of causes yet undreamed?
Hearing the robins calling, and calling it song?

Why not knowledge *and* happiness?
The question set me to imagining Paradise,
a place of slender trees that blossomed music,
A fascist loves impulse. I wanted logic.

Wikipedia said: **Paradise**: A place of harmony outside time.
But I wanted to earn my own sublime.

5. {Happiness possible in the USA?}

Where could I find Paradise in the United States?
I couldn't be hopeless and do it.
Recording the truth is never a mistake:
Oh my prideful boys and girls,
we've crooned praisesongs of enterprise and pluck.
While the Capitol scarved into a river of baroque pearls,
we've wandered a lonesome planet.

If you aren't succeeding, you will feel a lack.
Then you want to rediscover the old worn chair
and the simple retrograde of walking through a field
and the devotion of all your time to your feelings, sad sack,

faking your principles in return for health insurance,
skating on your despair.

6. {I question Dante's logic}

Reading *Paradiso*, the lustrous unreal,
I knew we were living in hell.
Children sold, women sold.
Slaughterings based on "affiliations,"
based on "grievance."
Humankind sworn enemy of humankind
and of an inflamed planet.

All of us planets, stuck in our orbits.
The Red Spot looked like an abstract painting on cold
Jupiter; in the Philippines, Marawi City ruined,
100,000 souls displaced in an "armed conflict"—

who were being punished for what, Dante,
on the crest of another July?

7. {Another July: everything cannot not change}

Another July: Every roundtrip ticket
from New York to London cost the Arctic
three square yards of ice.
The months without an *r* ticked,
heatened, wettened, flabbed. Diseases shook loose.
We rattled our triviality
into earthquakes. All we had learned from nature was fragility.

Weighed me down. Weighed us.
The citizenry was a listless witness,
choking. Lower than this we could not go.
But higher? The meter now is ticking and we owe . . .

I'd always been afflicted by vision.
Now I flashed and guessed: how to turn divine.

8. {Apotheosis}

Like a suspect slipped I down.
My sallow face flushed vermilion;
my estrogen and its volatiles receded;
receded my beliefs, my opinions;
a calm followed, strong.
We think our part is the whole, that's where we go terribly wrong.
Give me work, I said, something has to be done.

Like one acquitted did I rise.
Not blood-hot and personal: the world was fresh and general.
Everything cannot not change. Devise
another world, mellow and open and subtle?

What I'd been: a pinball struck, a knee tapped by a hammer,
struggling to understand, not struggling to care: a placeholder.

9. {Apotheosis, cont'd.}

Placeholder with small breasts, wide hips, alter-
ego sleepwalking, as if that were my job.
Now my job was faith, history, clarity of vision.
Like a goose I'd been stuffed with art, religion,
and chewed it up in a cozy prison.
Outside, I found a tiny brown pod,
infinitely detailed like a snail's shell, but vegetable, smaller

than a pearl, patterned with careful
nicks along the swirls. Why lavish detail
on such a trifle? I was detailed but wasn't special.
Around me, details abounded. My eyes burned to nail

it all down, see it whole. The work of a goddess:
I took my place.

10. {The Goddess confronts a country rooted in genocide, apocalypse}

On the road to the Last West, the taste for darnfool folk heroes
and Christ's fire-cloud coming survives.
You are not your professional experience.
You are not an audience for horrors.
Claws (systemic) rip at large incarcerated populations
and rip at all our lives.
I was a Goddess, sacred to the sorry, to deserving zeroes,

to those who square the dissonance, to those who in school did cry,
to those who integrate art into effectiveness, to the starers
at rivers, to the gesturers who come, bolder now, to the rescue. Pelted by
hail, I crossed the country with my femme-y power.

I thanked Louise, Gwendolyn, Anne for these stanzas, shorter.
And I cut clear through.

11. [Aerial establishing view}

I saw disease, endless war,
water shortages, rolling blackouts, opioids, arms,
noxious cynicism, soldiers who spoke in different
dialects and registers. Saw everywhere error
screened by gleam and grief;
saw someone believe just for a moment,
like the first bang, in real world liberation.

Saw it wasn't possible to become very rich without causing great harm.
Saw how wonder breaks through tedium to attention.
Zoom in: Saw a blue potato flower.
Thought. Saw that only the quality of the thought remains.

Offered up my superpower: my pain.
And I cut clear through.

12. {She sees}

I saw the slivered moon, lonesome and mournful;
saw a rack of miniskirts in American Apparel;
an unshaded bulb in an unshaded window;
people fucking without affection;
poems gone viral;
a doll with a home-crocheted apron;
an urn studded with lapis lazuli;

children with blood in their eyes.
A woman too alone said aloud, to God, *Was that really necessary? Fucker!*
Saw a good man do great things and no one learned from his mother.
Saw piles of unimportant objects; all the sentiments—

empathy gentler than anger; anger better than complacence.
I cut clear through.

13. {Police funeral}

Thousands of cops
jammed the barricaded midtown blocks.
What's happened at the tower, I thought, quailing.
For a goddess controls not human rages, bombs, rifles;
they are subject to chance, history, will.
What's going on, I asked a cop in hijab
under her cap. She answered: *Funeral.*

The streets full of heavy uniforms, armed; heavy feeling;
coffee shops where anger steamed.
The loudspeaker eulogy on loudspeaker chafing Fifth Avenue.
That's how the future seemed.

Don't look to a goddess to tell the future. In that crowd,
who could cut clear through?

14. *{Sees more, rejects noisy bombast}*

I went on, mothed north, south,
waited at bus stops with a slack mouth.
Saw an office where the emotionless always won;
at the seaside a gelatinous being slop onto my bare toes;
sperms meet eggs through true language, or its opposite, force,
or by dint of science. Saw a house sparrow glide on
air currents, her daughters simmering in the nest.

I went on, coasted east, west.
Saw epigenomes respond to environment.
Saw those who were nurtured recognize nurture.
Those who weren't, couldn't.

Purred a muted tune, that melody mine own thunder,
Zeus. And I cut clear through.

15. {Still she is Mommybody}

Even as Goddess who cut clear through,
the limits of my pants were the limits of my queendom.
Though I floated in my rainbow dress
an inch above the sidewalk, I heard requests:
What's up that skirt? What can you do with that tongue?
Slim of limb and wide of flank,
I was empty in the pants.

When I was a girl, in St. Ambrose Church,
a man's naked body hung, flexed.
I would grow into a receptacle, plastic and sexed,
on which a man's naked body with freedom

flexed. My skeleton a crucifix on which my parts hung.
I was a Goddess. Still I was Mommybody.

16. {Mommybody}

Why so voiceless, why so dim?
Mommybody drips with beauty.
Mommybody drains the energy.
And she thinks eternally of Him.

The systems are imperfect,
everyone would agree.
She held out a poem and asked
I made it, does it do, Nobodaddy?

Nobodaddy, overseer of all injustice.
She went on dates with Him.
He set her goals with vigor.
He filled her days with purpose.

The Holy Trinity is Our poetry,
he sounded: *Father Son Spirit*—
never to be understood but demonstrates
that He's fine with mystery.

He boomed: *I am mysterious because*
Secresy gains females loud applause.
—*What you think is the story is not the story,*
she whispered to Him, revelatory.

Like a god, everything magic
becomes science sooner or later.
Then becomes business. Mommybody
was forced to perform this, frantic.

First a rainbow hologram with eyes for nipples,
crowing and wet to the knees.
Next a calendar with mucus-y numbers.
Then: That'll be fifty cents a peek, please.

What was it like to be Mommybody?
It was like—I am so ugly! No, I am so beautiful!
It was like buying creams to make your face acceptable.
Exactly like. No, really.

But men groped and flashed and worse.
But other men held her when she cried
and one man called her labia neat as a crisply folded shirt.
Her faithful, so generously supplied.

She had good sex that gilded her with divinity,
bees in the belly dissolving, low, into honey,
and bad sex: He fingered her into yelps of pain that were not,
though He called them, pleasure. NOT.

Mommybody is divinely engineered.
Even with its thigh-fat, is her left leg
less than a suspension bridge?
Is her remaining egg less than an egg?

But in His Paradise, she is not goddess.
She is temptress and workhorse,
patched together with filth, rank jelly,
two balloons, things Mother said, teen movies.

Her Paradise is flexible and tough.
In her Paradise, she never smiles.
Her craggy face is honored.
Elsewhere, meanwhile,

Nobodaddy opened His mouth and (lying) spake:
You can be whatever you want to be. Pressured,
she thought a minute: *I would like to be Milton.*
Then she gave herself a shake:

No, I think I would like to be a person.
A person who lives kindly in a vicious system.
Ethics is the aesthetics of the future: right.
Each by her own body, each by her own light.

17. {Complication; imagination}

But must you complicate? Yes, I'm afraid I really must.
Disaster, if it comes, will lead to fifteen theories and six museums.
Built on unsound,
unstable ground!
Or else we are merely our debates. Trust
that our out-of-date political life, with Fidel on TV, was only material.
Trust the imagination, people!

Trust your fantasies of a puppy and its owlet pal,
lying down, feather to fur, in the soft hay.
Trust your memories of apples, a violet *shall*,
a chartreuse *yes*. Trust your wishes: disasters dialed back, a saner source.

Trust not, fear not apocalyptic discourse.
Let's cut clear through.

18. {The whole predicament}

I saw a mighty woman with a torch, whose flame
was the imprisoned lightning, and her name
Mother of Exiles. She promised Paradise.
Promised joy in chaos,
a spacious unbordering.
But I saw they liked their leaders authoritarian.
The soul in its perfection

becomes not less but more personal and individual.
I saw books, shine in them all:
Book of the Dead, Revelations, Analects, Koran, Testaments, Buddhist sutras.
I believed in imagery. I believed in disclosure.

Cassandra not my armature
but I believed we could change history's future.

19. {The love that moves the Sun and the other stars}

I found Paradise in a forest—no, a field—no, a park.
One of those greens that still greens in spring.
I removed my rainbow raiments and crowned
myself with clover. I lay myself naked on the laughing ground.
The Sun punctuated a sentence about love.
Around me slender trees. I heard a music made
of languages as many as were creatures to make sound.

They swore and joked and screamed and lied and lectured and prayed.
Paradise a long understanding which brings,
and is sometimes punctuated by, joy. A humor in the dark.
I dared to look into the light above.

I was taught that the Sun doesn't move at all.
But it does, it moves infinitesimally, and it doesn't fall.

20. {Dream of Paradise}

I found my happiness not in the optics,
a bit in the progress, a bit in the thinking,
sometimes in July, sometimes at lunch,
in the Paradise we made.
I found my happiness when each one gave,
when each one touched and each one wept.
I learned happiness when my questions were bleakest.

Happiness asked me to square the dissonance.
I found my happiness in a crumbling theater,
in a vulnerable text, in food glazed, and air,
sometimes in silence, in talk and in action,

often in nature and often with you,
in the Paradise we made.

21. {Her faithful ask:}

Will we attain Paradise? I don't understand the question!
Feeling and thinking are action, or forerunners of action.
Our feeling and thinking radicalize us.
We feel, we think, we accept the crisis.
You are a goddess, can you not advise us?
Pedestal not my best angle. My time so small.
I felt in waves my coming de-apotheosis. I spake:

TAKE WHAT YOU WANT, BUT TAKE JUST A LITTLE.
THOU SHALT NOT HATE THE BODY OF ANOTHER.
WE'RE A UNIVERSE OF BODIES ATTRACTING EACH OTHER.
THAT'S PARADISE, I said.

I imagined myself the mother of them all.
After, I was just a sweaty woman collapsed on a bed.

22. {Next day}

July:
A thin line of violet
stretches just above the black trees
across the silver sky.

Our fate
has what to do with that violet land?
The world is fresh and general—and late.
We care and we sometimes patiently don't understand.

Like a poem,
a god may be an interactive game
that depends on a believer
who searches with flexible aim.

Maybe I've just been talking to myself this whole time
or maybe I've earned my own sublime.

With imagination, inside our time,
maybe we'll earn our own sublime.

THE BELIEVER

I made a God. I called her Grace.
I said my prayers. I called them pleasure.
Pleasure her way to teach me pleasure.
Pleasure a stream and I a fish.

I made a God. I called her Grace.
I used no clay, no bronze, no iron.
I used my parts to make her whole.
And then I was part of the whole.

I found the others. I call them brave.
We laugh in the stream. We roll in the snow.
Our anger grows lilacs, our patience makes teeth.
The universe glows with oxytocin.

The Milky Way is part of the whole.
and we are part of the Milky Way.
The light makes a stream. The two streams flow.
The streams come together and we give birth.

We bathe our babies in the stream.
Babies we made and now they smile
at the God I made who I called Grace.
We say the prayers that are our pleasure.

Elizabeth Bishop, "In the Waiting Room"; "Chayote," Wikipedia; David Markson, *Reader's Block*; Jessica Bennett, Facebook comment; Elizabeth Bishop, "Large Bad Picture"; Joan Juliet Buck, "Coming of Age," *Harper's Bazaar*, April 28, 2015; Vladimir Mayakovsky, "An Extraordinary Adventure which Happened to Me, Vladimir Mayakovsky, One Summer in the Country"; Frank O'Hara, "A True Account of Talking to the Sun at Fire Island"; Dimitrios Psaltis, presentation at the Radcliffe Institute for Advanced Study, 2016; Alice Notley, *Sorrento*; John Skelton, *Armorie of Birds*; Heather Treseler, manuscript note; "Miniature Golf," Wikipedia; Robyn Selman, "Past Lives"; Mark Twain, *Adventures of Huckleberry Finn*; John Keats, "Ode to a Nightingale"; Gwendolyn Brooks, *Annie Allen*; William Blake, "To Nobodaddy"; Vladimir Lenin, attributed quote; *Justified*, final episode.

KATHLEEN OSSIP is the author of *The Do-Over*, a *New York Times* Editors' Choice; *The Cold War*, which was one of *Publishers Weekly*'s best books of 2011; *The Search Engine*, which was selected by Derek Walcott for the *American Poetry Review*/Honickman First Book Prize; and *Cinephrastics*, a chapbook of movie poems. Her poems have appeared in *Best American Poetry*, *Best American Magazine Writing*, the *Washington Post*, *Paris Review*, *Poetry*, *The Believer*, *A Public Space*, and *Poetry Review* (London). She teaches at The New School in New York, and has received a fellowship from the New York Foundation for the Arts.

SARABANDE BOOKS is a nonprofit literary press located in Louisville, KY. Founded in 1994 to champion poetry, short fiction, and essay, we are committed to creating lasting editions that honor exceptional writing. For more information, please visit sarabandebooks.org.

10/21